Real World
Colouring Book
For Advanced Users & Adults

Copyright 2019 By John Boom

50 Images

Created From Real Life Photos
For You To Colour As You Please.

ISBN 978-0-359-83337-5

9 780359 833375